David Martin's Re
He will be one c
parents who are

direct messages which saturate the different media
and contexts our children are exposed to, promoting
lifestyles that are both harmful and against the Creator's
intentions for us. He skilfully raises the key issues
at stake in the form of letters to his children before
applying the Bible to them and showing a much better
way. He helpfully reminds Christians of the dangers of
how we sometimes treat people with gender dysphoria
before challenging the assumptions made in the public
square about identity, authority, etc. This is no manual
from a detached observer but a plea from the heart of
someone seriously concerned for the well-being of his
own family and for the glory of God.

Andy Lines

Missionary Bishop to Europe of the Anglican Church in North
America

It is a sad reality that our young children are being
confronted with the transgender agenda. How are they
to understand and navigate an ideology that questions
our very biology—being made male and female? In a
very timely book David Martin provides some excellent
ways to talk to our children about this confusing issue.
David's approach is kind, caring and sensitive in
manner. I recommend this book to you.

Andrea Minichiello Williams

Co-Founder and Chief Executive of Christian Concern

David Martin has provided parents with a pastoral resource to equip children on a controversial and challenging topic in age-appropriate ways. Using language, metaphors, and themes that a child will understand, David helps establish a framework for biblical reflection on important themes such as creation, authority, brokenness, compassion, and sin. Parents can no longer sit out the transgender debate, and David's book is a useful tool to help parents bring the truths of God's Word to bear on a broken world.

Andrew T. Walker

Director of Policy Studies, the Ethics and Religious Liberty
Commission, Southern Baptist Convention,
author of *God and the Transgender Debate*

Here in London one of the schools we were thinking of sending our sons to has just approved a transgender uniform policy. My wife and I find ourselves ever more desperate to try and equip our children to navigate such a world, and we're so grateful to David Martin for this clearly Biblical and deeply practical response to a cultural wave all my family find profoundly confusing.

Rico Tice

Senior Minister (Evangelism), All Souls Church, London

David Martin has written a very gracious book about an extremely sensitive topic. The issue of transgenderism is one that is at the forefront of modern culture. It's certainly not a topic that we can just sweep under the rug and avoid, especially with our children. In the format of letters to his children, David helps parents everywhere consider how to graciously talk to their children about this issue. Parents, we need this book. Get it, read it, and then consider how to apply it to your conversations with your children.

Dave Furman

Senior Pastor of Redeemer Church of Dubai, author of *Being There* and *Kiss the Wave*

David Martin has written a book, comprised of letters to his four little children, that takes an emotionally fraught and politically explosive subject and transforms it into a lesson filled with love and hope …. While I take issue with David's conclusion, I do not with his process. The writing is exquisite, the sentiments are beautiful and I believe it is a wonderful guide for ALL parents in how to speak to little ones clearly, simply and with love, regardless of religious or non-religious belief.

Kris McDaniel-Miccio

Professor of Law & Fulbright Scholar, University of Denver Sturm College of Law

How do you love your transgendered neighbour? How do you speak loving truth with truthful love into such a complex issue? Wisely David Martin chooses the method of writing letters to his children, imagining their thoughts and questions. And as he does, he manages to be simple but never simplistic, honest but never harsh, biblical but never complicated. This book will certainly help parents to speak well with their children. But it also teaches all of us how to consider and then relate wisely and compassionately toward those who struggle with their gender.

Dr Andrew Collins

Biblical counsellor

REWRITING GENDER?

You, Your Family, Transgenderism and the Gospel

DAVID MARTIN

paperback ISBN 978-1-5271-0160-9
epub ISBN 978-1-5271-0253-8
mobi ISBN 978-1-5271-0254-5

First published in 2018 by
Christian Focus Publications Ltd,
Geanies House, Fearn, Ross-shire,
IV20 1TW, Scotland, U.K.
www.christianfocus.com

Cover design by Pete Barnsley
Printed by Bell & Bain, Glasgow.

Contents

To Caleb, Abigail, Clara and Daniel. With all my love and prayers that you may grow mature in Christ.

Introduction:
The Life of Po
(Why a book like this is necessary)

It was Clara's first trip to the cinema. She was going with her older brother and sister, and me. Thankfully, in our house going to the cinema is still a big deal, so there was lots of excitement beforehand. We bought the requisite popcorn, coke and sweets and settled down to watch the latest offering from Kung Fu Panda. I've enjoyed the previous two instalments and like Jack Black as an actor in general, so all my defences were down.

I'll not spoil the story for anyone who has yet to find a spare ninety-five minutes. Needless to say it did what so many 'children's movies' do so well today. It provided all the graphics, action and child-friendly humour that one has come to expect from Pixar and DreamWorks and yet combined it with enough subtleties suitable for adults to knowingly chuckle along with too. I have to admit I was lost in the moment.

It was only after, when I started reflecting on exactly what had happened to Po (the Dragon Warrior, Kung Fu Panda, star of the show) that my radar as a father and also as a Christian began to flash 'alert'. Setting aside the fact that there was an obvious Far Eastern spiritual push going on in the movie, as Po sacrificed himself to save his tribe, only to find that, in the spiritual world, he needed their help as much as they needed his. Even forgetting the fact that the whole story is carried along by the reality that Po now has two dads to look after him. Having been raised all his life by his adoptive father, Mr. Ping (a noodle cooking Swan Goose), Po's real father, Li Shan (a panda) makes an appearance, and they all have to navigate these new family dynamics. Right at the centre of all the action, however, is a less than thinly veiled appeal to the most sacred tenet of enlightened Western ideology today. Put simply this most sacred tenet insists that if we do nothing else in this life we must all 'be true to ourselves', whatever that means and whatever form that may take.

Now apart from having to leave the cinema once, occasioned by my eldest daughter Abigail's overconsumption of recently acquired Easter Eggs, we all had a thoroughly enjoyable afternoon. Caleb (my eldest son) did admit that he was slightly sad at Po's death, but overall, we had mindlessly, once again, drunk in a world view that at one point would have been completely foreign to the vast number of people.

Today, escaping into a spiritual netherworld; flexible, non-traditional family arrangements; and the constant drumbeat of achieving your true potential as decided by you, are nothing out of the ordinary. Indeed, identity itself today seems to be so mysterious and fluid that not even our physical bodies seem to be a sufficient pointer as to what or who we are. I don't want to sound like a crank so early on, but this has, of course, a very serious side to it. The blurred lines in the public square between freedom of speech, political correctness and intolerance make even the most informed person nervous when saying anything. In fact it especially makes the most informed person nervous to say anything. Specifically, in relation to the title of this book, the meteoric rise of the LGBT agenda can reduce the most ardent fundamentalist into silence.

This is part of the reason why (foolishly … obviously) I thought that it might be a good idea to sit down and start writing. I've never written a book before. I'm not even sure that I want to write a book, especially a book on such a subject as transgenderism (and especially transgenderism in relation to children). I'd far rather be sitting zoning out with my wife watching more mindless TV, than set out on a venture that could possibly end in the loss of some friends. But then, I think about my children and the 'brave new world' they are growing up in. It is a world totally different to anything I ever knew. I suppose that is part of the reason why I am writing this book; to try and understand that world a little better. However, the main reason I think it needs writing is to try and give us all some handles and signposts as our children grow into teenagers and then set out themselves as adults (and prayerfully as Christians) into this ever evolving mix of flexible family arrangements and DIY gender.

Let me issue the customary disclaimer at this point and tell you what this book is not. It is not seeking to provide you with a bang-up-to-date survey and analysis of all that the scientific community are saying about

11

transgenderism. This, I know, has already gone through some evolutions and I am not totally certain exactly how different regulatory bodies are classifying it at present. Neither is it a book that will give you a detailed textual analysis on all the relevant scriptural passages. I do have Bible references included at the end of each chapter, but this is for your own personal reflection and further reading. What the book tries to do is to follow the overarching storyline of the Bible in an attempt to make it clear that transgenderism is a symptom of a far deeper problem that only Jesus can heal. He alone is loving enough not only to get involved in our lives, but to give Himself for us, and He alone is powerful enough not simply to change our own self-estimation, but our very nature itself. Each chapter is a letter written to one of my children and seeks therefore to think through the issue from their point of view.

Granted, my children are not likely to pick this up and read it in the next five to ten years. Caleb is currently 9, Abigail is 7, Clara is 5 and Daniel is 3. I'd be very surprised if they ever want to read something I've written, given they never want to listen to a word I usually say at present. So, therefore, I am actually writing for parents, and especially parents with young children. I'm trying to imagine our children's questions and seek to answer them with words and language that they will be able to grasp.

Almost nothing is as it was, and therefore the more we realise this as Christians the better equipped we will be at engaging our family and friends and wider culture with the only news that will, in the end, bring about real, lasting life transformation.

1
A Scary Dream

Dear Caleb,

I've just read another story today in a magazine that I found very difficult. It was not difficult in the sense that I couldn't understand it. It was difficult because it talked about people, very young people about your age, who see themselves very differently from the little babies they were born. There was one story of a boy who did not want to grow up to be a man, and a girl who did not want to grow up to be a woman. Instead this boy wanted to become a girl and grow up as a woman, and the girl wanted to become a boy and grow up to be a man.

Now the first thing I want to say is that if this sounds strange, don't be alarmed. Many of the doctors who are trying to help these boys and girls are themselves not sure what is the best thing to do for them. There are some things that even grown-ups are confused about. (I'm going to write to you about being a mummy and daddy and a doctor, even though I am not one myself, in another letter soon.)

Secondly, since you may sometimes have to think about these things in your classroom and with your friends, please never be afraid of asking me your biggest and toughest questions. If I don't know the answer, I will do my best to find one; one that comes as close to the truth as possible. Remember what I've always said? If we lie to one another, we cannot trust one another, and if we cannot trust one another then we cannot be friends. That would just be awful. You should never be afraid of asking questions and I love to hear what you are discovering as you grow up. Life is such a great adventure, with many surprises along the way.

Thirdly, and this is very important, as confusing and as difficult as you may find these ideas about boys and girls, always remember that behind these ideas are real people. We are talking about boys and girls, many of whom are very scared themselves. I think at times it must feel like they and their families are living in a scary dream, only in reverse. They live it when they are awake and go to sleep to try and escape it, but it is right there when they wake up each morning again. So never ever make fun of them or join with the crowd who might be bullying them. You may even need to tell some people who say hurtful things to be quiet.

And lastly for now, and this is the most important thing, never forget that God made the world and that no matter what He loves it. Like every most important thing, I'm going to have to say more about this than I can put into one letter right now. But remember that God does not want to see anyone get hurt or indeed see people hurting one another. God loves this world so much, in fact, that He sent His Son, Jesus, into the world to show us exactly what He is like. So as we live in His world, try and see them and treat them in the same way that Jesus has treated you. That way you will show everyone that you know what God is like. He loves to treat us with love. That love can be tough love at times and we may not always like what He says or does in our lives, but we know that He knows best. Be patient, be kind, try to forget your own wants and desires and put others first, and remember that Jesus has promised to be always with you. Stick close to Him. Copy Him. And don't worry if people sometimes laugh or even reject you as you try to follow Him.

Lots of love,
Dad

~ Psalm 16; Matthew 11:28-30; John 3:16, 15:18-16:4;
Philippians 4:8-9 ~

● ● ● ● ● ● ● ● ● ● ● ● ● ● ●

Your children are going to have to learn how to live with people who are totally unlike them. How they live with them is the subject of this book. Given the considerable push in the media at present to advocate for a fluidity in gender, this is going to mean that they will have questions about themselves and others they meet. The natural 'childish' reaction is to stereotype and then treat others with disdain. The burden of this first letter is to help Caleb (9) see that whilst a Christian cannot accept the cultural affirmation of transgenderism, we cannot either, as Christians, simply treat others who are different to us with contempt, condemnation or condescension. Our first approach must be as those who have been shown divine compassion, to extend similar compassion to others.

How to begin a conversation:

- *The letter begins by talking about something I read in a newspaper to do with transgenderism. If you watch TV at all with your children the likelihood is that something around gender is going to flash across the screen. Think how you might respond to this beforehand.*
- *When talking about class friends in school listen carefully to how your son/daughter speaks about them, and try and help them to see that other children might be struggling with questions about identity and being part of the crowd. Perhaps as you read stories together highlight how lonely some children can feel at times.*
- *Get a chalkboard and put some of the verses at the end of this letter up for your whole family to see. Talk about how this should shape the way we see ourselves and the world around us today.*

Prayer ideas:

Our loving heavenly Father, thank you that because of Jesus we get to be part of your family. This is such a great privilege. Help us each day to see more and more that we do not belong to the world, our friends, or even to ourselves, but that we belong to you. Amen.

2
Play Dough: A Love/Hate Relationship

Dear Clara,

I know you love the stuff. Play dough. It feels nice when you squeeze it through your fingers. The colours are so bright and the smell is rather pleasant too. Actually, I have to admit that I do quite like the smell, but Clara you also know that this is where my liking of play dough ends.

When you reach for it and bring it off the shelf I know that this means only one thing for the rest of the day. Your mummy and I will be peeling it off the table, scraping it from the chairs and watching in horror as you tramp the stuff all through the house. I know for you it is all part of the fun but for us it is part of the problem. The other thing I find so annoying is what actually goes back into those tubs. You may think I'm being too strict, a little bit crazy even, but when a yellow, that used to be like the colour of a daffodil, is now murky brown like a muddy puddle, that really annoys me. Or when that blue that used to be as blue as the sky is now a swirl of random colours, like a rainbow rolled into a ball, I mean really! You love it, but it doesn't really help your brother with his colour recognition!

Clara, these letters that I'm writing to you have to do with something far more serious than playing with play dough, and yet I think that when it comes to talking about boys who want to grow up to be girls and girls who want to grow up to be boys, what you can do with play dough is a good example of what they want to do with their bodies. The big word that people are using to talk about this is transgenderism. That is a very long word, so please don't worry if you cannot use it or even say it properly yet. Just remember that we are talking about boys and girls who are deeply sad that they have been born either as a girl or a boy.

This will not be the case for many boys and girls. Many boys and girls, if not most, are very happy that they get to be a boy or a girl. But for some boys, they feel like a girl trapped inside a boy's body and for some girls they feel like a boy trapped in a girl's body. This, as you can imagine, is very confusing for them and so they want to try and fix this. We'll talk more about this in another letter.

For now, I think it is important for you to see that this problem takes us right back to the start, to when we were born. In fact, it takes us right back to the start of the Bible's story too, when God made two people right at the very beginning. Right at the start God made a man called Adam and He made a woman called Eve. We'll talk more about them in another letter, but what you will see in their story is something that is true for all our stories. God makes each one of us. He made you and your brothers and sister. He made Mummy and He made me. He made everyone you will ever meet. That means He loves us and cares for us all.

To make things even better, when you look at the Bible you'll see that God does not make the same person twice ... ever. This means that you are special, and therefore specially loved by God, just like He loves each and every other person you'll ever meet. This, Clara, by the way, is why you should treat everyone you ever meet with kindness and respect too.

However, while God makes everyone and makes everyone special, God's original plan, which still stands for almost everyone, is that He makes us either as a boy or a girl, and what I mean by that is that He gives us either a boy's body or a girl's body. Since He makes them both, both are just as special and valuable to Him. In fact, right at the very beginning He said that if the world was filled only with boys there would be something seriously missing, and if it was filled only with girls there would be something seriously missing too.

So what happens when a boy feels that he is actually more like a girl or when a girl thinks she actually should be a boy?

Well remember the play dough? A boy who is happy to be a boy is like one complete ball of, let's say, blue play dough, because that's simply the colour that most people think of when they think about boys ... There is nothing but blue in the way they are made, and the way they think about themselves is exactly the same. Likewise for a girl who is happy being a girl; when the way she has been made and how she feels are the same, it's like one complete ball of, let's say, pink play dough. But what happens to someone who is born a boy, for example, but sees himself more as a girl? Well, that ball of play dough is now mixed up between blue and pink. They have been made one way but feel they should actually look totally different, the opposite in fact to the way they have been made.

If the whole truth was told, Clara, actually, many boys have some bits of pink mixed in and enjoy things that some people say only girls should like and many girls have some bits of blue mixed in too and enjoy doing what some say only boys should like. You can see this in your mummy and me. She likes shooting and wearing her wellie boots and I like drinking coffee and drawing, but just because a boy might like girlie things and a girl might like boyish things, doesn't actually change them from a boy into a girl or from being a girl into a boy. We'd love you to grow up and enjoy all sorts of things in life, and since you've been made as a girl to enjoy them as a girl.

The problem for some boys and girls is that their feeling of sadness at being a boy trapped inside a girl's body or a girl inside a boy's body, is so strong that they want to change even how they have been made. It is like taking that ball of different coloured play dough, of blue and pink, and trying to pull it apart in order to connect it to another piece of play dough of the same colour. This, as you well know, is not so easy to do.

Not only is it not easy (and can be especially difficult for their mummies and daddies to watch), but it also deep down says to God that He got it wrong in making that little boy a boy, or that little girl a girl. So whilst it may give those boys and girls who want to change how they look to match how they feel some sort of happiness, ultimately it makes God sad. He has given them a wonderful gift in their bodies, just like He has given you a wonderful gift in your body, but just because they don't like how it feels they want to exchange their gift for something else.

You need to know, Clara, that even many grown-ups are confused by this, including me in certain ways. It is very distressing to even read of some of their stories and you will need to be a really good listener if you should ever meet a boy or girl who is trying to cope with these problems.

Sadly, if you were to answer them with what I have just said in this one brief letter, you may not be listened to just as well. In fact, some people might even stop being your friends. You will need to be strong, even as a girl, because many people will disagree with you. But, Clara, please treat everyone with respect and love and never be afraid of the truth as you do so.

All my love,
Dad.

~ Genesis 1-2, 6:5-6; Exodus 20:1-17; Job 38-40:5;
Psalm 8, 19, 139; Hosea 11:1-11; Matthew 19:1-6;
Luke 1:26-80; Ephesians 5:15-33 ~

● ● ● ● ● ● ● ● ● ● ● ● ● ● ●

Identity obviously is one of the key issues in all our conversations about transgenderism. However, more importantly than this is the simple fact that we are not just having a conversation about an idea or an -ism, but about real people's lives. This was one of the main reasons I thought a book like this needed to be written. This letter to Clara (5) seeks to explain the Biblical approach to gender identity and the terrible confusion and pain that those living with gender dysphoria must have. Rooted in the very essence of creation are two simple ideas that the world cannot accept or hold together at present. First, we are all made equal by God. He does not love one gender better than the other. But secondly, men and women have been made to be different from one another. Both have their own special roles to fulfil in God's grand plan. And of course what we see is that men and women are interdependent in fulfilling each of their respective roles. Setting this picture of reality before our children has never been more important. It is key for us all to see our loving God's original intention is that we are to live sympathetically and yet uncompromisingly with others.

While we see God's good design is to create individuals either as male or female, some individuals are born intersexed. It is critical to acknowledge these biological facts and, as the message of this book emphasises, to treat everyone with compassion. In such cases where a biological fact requires a decision, with professional help and family pastoral care, inevitably it is a choice for the person concerned, one way or the other. In the absence of such biological factors forcing a decision, the desire to change ones biological sex is driven by ideological and cultural agendas which this book is seeking to unmask, challenge and oppose as sensitively as possible.

How to begin a conversation:

- Don't wait for your children to see the grandeur and beauty and mystery and power of creation. Talk regularly about the might and splendour of God in all that He has made. I'm sure we all will have seen at least one episode of Blue Planet II *(Sir David Attenborough's latest offering)*.

- Be sure to help your children to respect their own bodies as boys and as girls and as will happen during bath times, for example, using age appropriate language, don't be afraid of affirming the difference between them as a girl and their brother as a boy. The important thing here is simply not to make a big deal of it. It's just natural.

Prayer ideas:

Dear God, you are so awesome and powerful. You made everything and it all belongs to you. You made me and my family and I'm so thankful for them all. Help us as a family to love one another and to love you and love reading your Word, the Bible. Amen.

3
A Lamp, a Light & the Love of God

Dear Abigail,

As I thought about what I wrote to your sister last time, I can see the need to take a step back and explain where some of my thoughts come from. I can remember when I was growing up that if my big brother told me to do something that I didn't want to do, like tidy my room or wash the dishes, I would shout straight back at him, 'Who says so?' I certainly wasn't going to do it if it was only his bright idea.

As you grow up this will be a question you will need to ask yourself time and time again. I want to encourage you to only ever think a certain way or change the way you actually behave when you are absolutely happy that you know who it is that is giving you the instructions; that you trust them. Lots of people simply follow the crowd, but that is not always the best course of action.

As I said, when it comes to this subject of transgenderism especially, it is important to remember that even the experts are confused, so don't think that you must accept the most up-to-date scientific discovery as being the final answer. The latest news is not always the greatest news.

In fact, for thousands of years, millions of people have been living their lives based on a very ancient book. While some people have misunderstood it, this book has done more good in the world than perhaps any other book. It is of course the Bible.

Now the Bible is a big book. Well, it's not a book really at all! The Bible is actually an entire library of books, written over many, many centuries, by a whole bunch of people, some from very different cultures indeed. What is amazing, however, is that in the Bible you can easily trace one big story from start to finish. (My other letters will try and show you how it fits together and why it is so helpful for everyone, not just for those who are confused about being a boy or a girl.) Since it has been written by so many people from so many different places yet contains one big story, that might suggest the real author is bigger than time, and not restricted to just one part of the world. This is, at the end of the day, what the Bible says about itself. It says that God chose people to write it, but He made sure that what they said was exactly what He wanted us to know.

Think about it like this. You know that I love your mummy. You know that I love her, because I buy her flowers … sometimes. We have a date night … occasionally. I take you away for a few hours so she can have some mummy time to herself. But actually one of the best ways I can show your mummy that I love her is by talking with her, listening to her and discovering how she feels about the things I do for her. I can do a lot of things for her, but if I never talk to her, and if I do not mean what I say when I do talk to her, then she will not know an awful lot about who I really am and why I do the things I do for her. Abigail, it is because I love your mummy that I talk to her and mean what I say.

Exactly the same is true when we come to think about God. If God is loving, one of the clearest ways He can love us is to say what He means and to mean what He says. It would be a very unloving thing for God to speak in any way that was confusing or unclear. It would be worse if He kept the truth from us, and even worse still if He were to lie to us. That type of god would not just be unloving. At the end of the day we couldn't even trust him. But when you open the Bible, you know already from the bits you have read, that it is clear. The Bible is an example of God's love.

Also if He is a truly loving God, then we would expect Him to be the clearest in what He says on that which matters most to us, or should matter most to us. So when it comes to a question like—'Did Jesus really come from heaven?'—that is an important issue and the Bible is absolutely clear. He did, making Him totally unique in the history of the world. Or if treating others with respect matters, again you'd expect the Bible to be clear on this and it is. But when it comes to a question such as, did He make each one of us to be a boy or a girl? This is where it gets very confusing for some people today. On such an important question, however, the Bible is clear. As I said God is indeed the one who made each one us and gives us life either as a boy or a girl. It may not be the life we want or like, but that is another matter, and we'll talk about that in another letter. But it would be terrible if we had to make up our own reason for being here in the world; if we had no clue why we were here, or even worse still who we were actually meant to be. In all of this God has not left us in the dark. Our bodies are wonderful gifts from God telling us who He wants us to be, and the Bible is another amazing gift of love from our loving God explaining clearly what it means to be a boy or a girl.

The Bible actually does talk about itself as a lamp and a light; two very helpful things if you are in a dark place. But many grown-ups today, however, think the opposite about the Bible. Especially when it talks about what it means to be a boy or a girl, many people think that the Bible actually leads us into darkness and blinds us to the truth about ourselves: about what it means to be a man or woman. But this, Abigail, is simply another example that many grown-ups are still asking that question, 'Who says so?' The answer the Bible gives is that 'God tells us who we really are made to be in His Word. In other words, 'He says so'. It is one of the most loving things He can do and has done for us.

Abigail, as you grow up you do need to make up your own mind on all sorts of stuff. In other words you need to decide what you think on important and difficult subjects like this. As you make up your mind, however, please let me assure you that you can trust the Bible, because ultimately behind it all is a God of love.

With all my love,

Dad

~ Psalm 119:73-80, 105-112; Isaiah 55:8-13; Ezekiel 37;
Mark 4:1-20; Luke 7:1-10; John 1:1-18, 6:60-69;
James 1:19-21 ~

● ● ● ● ● ● ● ● ● ● ● ● ●

Authority is just as important as identity in the wider conversation about transgenderism. This letter written to Abigail (7) explains why we can indeed trust God's Word. Almost everyone, if they are prepared to believe in a god at all, will want to agree at some point that he should be a god of love. Thankfully, the Christian God is love. As part of this love He communicates clearly with us on the issues that matter most to us. So, therefore, His Word can be trusted. Having young children, any parent sees first hand that the essence of sin is to mistrust and reject the authority over them. As adults we all still labour under the same condition. The world wants to do all it can to silence God's Word on the subject of human sexuality at the moment by treating the Bible as dangerous and repressive. The opposite could not be more true.

How to begin a conversation:

- *Open your Bibles regularly as a family. Talk about what they are learning in Sunday school.*
- *Practice what you preach!*
- *Read them stories about those whom God has used down through church history to bring blessings to the world.*
- *Point out how wrong the world gets it when it turns its back on God's Word.*

Prayer ideas:

Gracious God, thank you that you are a speaking God and have not left us in the dark. Help us to read, understand and walk in the light of your Word more and more each day. Amen.

4
Building Lego in the Dark

Dear Caleb,

I said at the end of my last letter that the Bible is like a lamp and a light. This is both a wonderful thing and at the same time a rather terrifying thing. Wonderfully, the Bible shines in our world, even today. It's wonderful because without light we would all die. You're learning a little bit about this in school as you discover the power of the sun. It gives us light and heat and produces life. The Bible is like that in our hands. But the Bible is also a very annoying thing too, and many people today think that it is actually quite dangerous. The reason why some people think it is annoying is because it chases away the darkness in our lives and takes away any excuse for our mistakes. This makes it dangerous as well because it actually says that the way we think and behave today is so wrong.

It is a little bit like that big stone you lift at the beach or in the garden. When you lift that stone what do you find? Well, you usually find all those little sea shrimps or bugs that love the darkness. When you lift the stone they start running away from the light. Why? Well probably because, for one thing, they are scared. They're hiding in the darkness because they know if they come into the light, they will be in great danger. That is the way that many people react to the Bible, because like all those little creatures who would rather live in the darkness, doing their own thing, we know if we step into the light we might not really like what we see and have to admit that we are in fact wrong.

It wasn't always like this. You may remember the first two chapters in the Bible that talk about God's perfect creation. Everything was in perfect harmony. There was a great peace in the world. And God's wonderful creation all fitted together like one of those amazing Lego creations that you love to build. The opening chapters of the Bible are so important because they tell us not only what God is like, but what the world should be like too. In that world there was no confusion, no pain, no loneliness. Well, Adam was alone, but not in the sense that he felt lonely. What I mean is that Adam alone was not able to fully reflect God or fulfil the job God had in mind for him and so God in His kindness made the perfect missing piece for him. Eve, the perfect woman, was the missing part in God's jigsaw masterpiece. And for the first two chapters no one was lost. Everyone knew their place and fitted beautifully together. Adam and Eve knew who they were themselves and were content. Adam and Eve knew 'whose' they were and were happy.

Then something totally tragic happened. A tragedy is when something beautiful is ruined, or when something perfect is broken. It's like when that wonderful Lego creation you have just finished crashes to the floor and bursts into a hundred little pieces. This is what some grown-ups call the Fall.

And this is the world that we now live in today. It is not perfect. It is far from perfect. Remember I've taught you so many times that it is beautiful, but it is also terribly broken as well. And just as if things could not get any worse, imagine that as your great Lego creation crashes to the floor, at that very moment, the lights suddenly go out. This is where the darkness comes in. So essentially you are now blind and without instructions as to how to put it back together again. How would you feel? This is the trouble that everyone in the world is in today. Our lives are like those Lego pieces now, and we are all trying (some desperately) to put them together again without the instructions, in the dark. So when the Bible is opened and it shines a light on what we look like, well, it can be very painful to see the uncomfortable truth about ourselves.

Essentially, none of us have it 'together' as much as we like to think we do. And more worryingly none of us like to be told that who we are is unacceptable to God.

This is very important to remember about everyone you will ever meet, including yourself. Oh, you are beautifully and wonderfully made, but you are also broken and cannot fix yourself.

This is especially important to remember when you meet boys who perhaps used to be girls, or girls who perhaps used to be boys. They are trying to put their lives together in a way that makes most sense to them. It can be, and usually is, very confusing for them and for their mummies and daddies too. Remember that scary dream! So again, please don't ever laugh at them, or please don't ever be afraid to be friends with them either. You know that when you have a scary dream you want either your mummy or me to stay with you. It would be terrible to have to walk through life, living that scary dream, with no one to turn to.

Here's the big point to this letter, Caleb: without the Bible all of us are in the dark about who we really are, and when we open the Bible it shows us that none of us can fix ourselves. No one is any better than anyone else. There is only one person who ever lived that was perfect in every way, but He is so great I'll need to write a whole new letter just about Him.

Before that, I know what I have said in this letter is actually very difficult. It is hard to understand, but even when you do understand it, it is even more difficult to accept. Please do talk to me more about this as you grow up, as I have struggled to accept it. But as I said in my previous letter to your sister, the Bible is crystal clear on the really important matters, and it could not be more clear than it is on this one thing: we like the darkness more than the light and cannot fix who we are by ourselves.

If the truth be known, we all live scary dreams at times and go to sleep to escape them.

Love you with all my broken love,
Dad

~Genesis 3; Exodus 32:1-8; Judges 21:25; Psalm 14:1-2; Ecclesiastes 1:16-18; Jeremiah 2:12-13; Matthew 7:24-28; John 3:16-21; Romans 1:18-2:10, 3:9-20 ~

• • • • • • • • • • • •

Having established the background this chapter seeks to explain why we are in such confusion today about identity and also underscore that the rejection of God's Word is an example of our unwillingness to see things from His perspective. We all find this so difficult because the perspective that the Bible gives us about ourselves is that none of us will ever be able to fix ourselves. Each and every one of us lives with a deep and sometimes unacknowledged sense of our own imperfections. The main point in relation to transgenderism is that this painful reality is something all too real for those who struggle with who God has made them. Caleb (9) is just learning that this world is not only beautiful, but also profoundly broken, and that we need someone totally different from anyone else if we are going to see our way through.

How to begin a conversation:

- *When correcting your own child's bad behaviour, ask why they are acting in such a way; trying to uncover the disobedience not only of their actions, but of their hearts. Emphasise deep down we all want to live our own way without accepting the authority that is over us.*
- *Helping our children realise that this is a world under God's curse will help them be realistic when they are confronted with tragedy and disappointment. Talk about things that make you sad or frustrated. Such things point us to our need for Jesus more and more.*

Prayer ideas:

Our great God, we know that there is so much that upsets, confuses and angers us in the world. How much more then must your heart break? Please help us see our own sinful ways and as those who are in need of forgiveness, be quick to point others to Jesus and forgive them too. Amen.

5
It's Microscopes, not Mirrors, that Are Really Important

Dear Clara,

I'm so impressed that you are able to clean your teeth and brush your own hair already! And it certainly won't be too long until you're tall enough to see into the mirror all by yourself.

I actually heard something the other day that didn't seem to be quite right. When it comes to mirrors, men actually spend more time using them than women! I'm not sure if I heard it properly, but I'm sure that most men would not agree. Then I started counting how many mirrors we actually have in our house. I reached eight or nine and then gave up counting. There are only six people in our house and yet we have more than enough mirrors for us all.

Clara, this seems to me to be something of a problem and as you grow up it could turn into a big trap. I see it especially when I'm looking at a photograph someone has taken that includes me. No matter who else is in the picture, the person I spend most time looking at is … myself! It is embarrassing to admit it, but even should the photograph be of us as a family, the one person I look for first is not you or any of your brothers or sister, it is not even your mummy, but as painful as it is to admit it, the first person I look for is myself.

We live and you are going to grow up in a world that is terribly obsessed with 'outward appearance'. That means that 'how you look', 'what clothes you wear', 'the condition of your skin', 'the colour of your hair', 'the tone of your tan' matter almost more than anything else. To make matters worse, if you don't have the *right* look, or wear the *latest* clothes, or have the *slightest* blemish, then you may find that some of your friends can be actually quite cruel and cut you out from certain games or groups. This is terribly painful and the hurt can last a long, long time. You will obviously want to try to make sure that such a thing never happens to you, and if it does you will want to make certain changes to make sure that such a thing never happens again.

At this point, however, you have a choice to make. It will seem like a very difficult choice to make the first couple of times, but the more you make it, then perhaps the easier it will become. The choice is between mirrors or microscopes! Now that will sound really quite strange, so let me explain.

You know what a mirror does? It shows you 'how you look' on the outside. This, as I said, is the main way in which most people think about themselves today. If they look good on the outside, then they feel good about themselves on the inside. We all do it, and we must take good care of our bodies, but it is so easy then to think that this is what matters most. In fact, this is often the case when it comes to boys who want to be girls and girls who want to be boys. Some boys and girls are so unhappy with what they see on the outside that they decide to make such big changes so as to become completely different to the way they were born. For them, however, they are not trying to make friends with other people. As strange as it will sound, they are actually trying to make friends with themselves. They feel as if there is a different person living on the inside to the one they see on the outside. I know this is very hard to understand, but you must try hard to understand it. They want to change the way they look and they want to change so much about the way they look or else they will feel so sad.

This, surprisingly for many, is where the Bible can be such a great help because it asks us to think differently about what is important. Remember I said that the Bible shows us that none of us is acceptable to God, and worse still that none of us can fix ourselves or change ourselves enough to make that any better. That sounds like bad news, and it is. But where the Bible begins to speak 'good news' into our lives is when it begins to teach us what matters most to God. And you'll know from some of the stories in the Bible that God thinks quite differently about us when He looks at what matters. It is not just what we look like on the outside that He thinks is important. In fact, what we look like on the outside is, at the end of the day, of very little importance to God. What He considers to be of the greatest importance is 'what we look like on the inside'. And this is where you need to look at your life, not simply with a mirror, but with a microscope.

So let me ask you if you know what a microscope does? A microscope is usually used to look at very small things that are on the 'inside' of something. In other words, a microscope looks at what things are really made of. Now, when I say that you need to use a microscope to look at your life, not just a mirror, I don't mean that you should take off your ear and put it under the microscope, or stick out your tongue and try to look at it under a microscope. You would look very silly if you tried to do that. No, what I want you to see is that it is your attitudes, what you like and don't like, your feelings toward others, how you treat your friends and more importantly how you treat your enemies that really counts. Above all else you need to be sure that you love God first and treasure what He has done for you.

Some day, I know this is incredibly hard to understand at the minute, but some day you will grow up and get a lot taller, even as tall as Mummy and Daddy, and then some day, a long time from now, you will even get to be as old as Granny and Grandpa. Then, try as much as you like, you will not be able to make yourself as young and beautiful as you are now. All you will be left with is your character. Your character is what you are like on the inside; the type of person that you really are. It is something that can get better and more beautiful with age.

So make sure that you keep a close eye on how you look on the inside! Give it as much attention as you spend looking at your hair and face in the mirror. Maybe give it even more attention, for this is what is really going to last. It doesn't even really matter if you

40

grow up to become a train driver who enjoys reading science books and watching action movies. Neither does it matter if your brothers grow up to become ballet dancers who enjoy painting and quiet nights in. The most important question is, do you love God and love what He has done for you? Do you know that God loves you? Do you know what He has done to prove that love? Then regardless of how you look, you can know, Clara, you are loved.

You are you know … loved!
Dad

~1 Samuel 16:1-7; Esther 2:7, 9, 15-16, 4:1-17; Proverbs 5:1-6, 11:22; Isaiah 53:2-3; Matthew 9:9-13; 2 Corinthians 5:6-10; Galatians 2:20; 1 Peter 3:3-7 ~

● ● ● ● ● ● ● ● ● ● ● ●

This chapter seeks to debunk some of the modern narratives that have led to the situation we find ourselves in today, focusing on one popular idea that 'image is everything'. It also points to what is really important in God's eyes, namely our character and relationship with Him. Clara (5) is already bombarded daily with the pressure to dress in a way that will express how she is feeling, empower her and ensure that she is prettier than everyone else. For those living with transgenderism this is an even greater problem, as they seek to resolve their feelings with how they look, but it is not going to be resolved by simply changing their appearance either.

How to begin a conversation:

- If grandparents are on the family scene and you are able to extol their virtues, point your children to their kindness, generosity and love. Perhaps even when turning through the pages of an old photo album, talk about the character of those you're looking at.
- Take opportunities to talk regularly about how your children are treating others, especially those who are different in appearance and emphasise the Christian way of grace and truth.
- When it comes to going to parties or giving presents, should they always be wrapped in plastic and shiny paper, or might you be able to point your children to see that what mummy would really like for her birthday is a small act of kindness?

Prayer ideas:

Dear heavenly Father, thank you for showing us in your Word what you are really looking for in us and please help us not to be carried away by how we look on the outside. In Jesus' name, Amen.

6
Will the Real 'Me' Please Sit Down!

Dear Daniel,

I wrote a letter to your sister last time, asking her (and you too) to make sure you think carefully about what matters most in this life. Some people want to get rich and have really fast cars. Some people want to be popular and join the celebrity ranks. Others want to be young and stay beautiful forever. None of these are awfully bad hopes and dreams, but all of them are actually not very important.

I also mentioned that what matters most to most of us, is not what matters most to God. For most people, how they look is a really important thing. For many people it is one of *the* most important things. But when God looks at us, He wants to see what we are like on the inside (our character).

Like in another letter I wrote, this is both a good thing and at the same time a deeply troubling thing. It is good in that the pressure is off us since we do not always have to look our best. We need to teach our mirrors a lesson and tell them that they do not rule over our feelings.

But it is also troubling because we have a far harder job changing what we are like on the inside.

You will already know that no matter how hard you try, it is really difficult to share your toys with others. It is also incredibly difficult to always do what your mummy and I tell you to do. And you cannot but feel jealous when someone in class wins a prize, gets a better score in a test, or simply has more friends than you do. That's because inside us all is a thirst to be at the centre of all the action. I've heard the words come out of my mouth so many times when I tell you, 'You are not at the centre of this house,' and feel a little ashamed, because I know how selfish I can be too.

The painful fact is that we all wish that we could change something about the life we have been given to live. How many times in a day do you think your sister says to me, 'It's just not fair!', or your brother shouts: 'But why … ?'

Actually, when your mummy and I first got married, for at least the first year, I would regularly have to admit to her that I didn't like myself very much at times, because I saw just how selfish I really could be.

And although it is not exactly the same, perhaps for many of those boys who want to change to become girls and girls who want to change to become boys, they live with this frustration too.

It may surprise you to hear me say this, but for some of these boys and girls they are right in their deep desire to change who they are. In their desire to change, they are in some ways just like everyone else. If only they could change this or that, then life would be more bearable. If only these set of circumstances were different, then life would be happier.

But what is perhaps even more surprising to hear is that their deep desire to change does not go anywhere nearly deep enough. In fact for many boys who change to become girls and many girls who change to become boys, when they eventually do grow up they still suffer from deep deep sadness, even though they have made such a big big change. This is because none of us can make enough changes in our lives so that we will eventually be happy and content forever more.

Daniel, someone else must change us on the inside and I think in my next letter it is about time that I told you about Him.

Lots of love,
Dad

~ *Genesis 6:9, 9:20-21; Deuteronomy 32:48-52; Jeremiah 7:9, 31:33-34; Romans 7:7-25; James 4:4-10* ~

• • • • • • • • • • • • • • •

Transgenderism in one sense is simply just another way for people to express the fact that they know something is not right with this world. It is a deep truth we must all come to terms with. Thankfully, God knows this too and has not left us to ourselves. But, as well as sympathising with those with gender dysphoria, as Christians we want everyone to see that the answer does not lie within. This is where true life change begins. When we realise that God is not just interested in outward appearance, but what we are like on the inside. What we are like on the inside, however, is far from perfect, and so at last we will see our need for a saviour.

How to begin a conversation:

- *Almost everything you hear, read or watch with your children will be sending them the same message today: 'Whatever you do, be true to yourself!' Talk about the trouble you've seen when you've been true to yourself, and why it is not always the best course of action.*
- *Being selfish comes naturally to us all. This is something your children will be only too familiar with. Ask them to consider how they feel when they see others being selfish. Try and contrast this with what it means to be generous instead.*

Prayer ideas:

Dear God, the good news of Jesus teaches us that we are more wicked than we could actually imagine and yet at the very same time more loved than we could ever possibly hope. Thank you for Jesus. Amen.

7
All the King's Horses and All the King's Men

Dear Abigail,

It's your birthday tomorrow! You'll be seven years old and along with every other parent who watches their children grow up, I simply cannot believe that you are already so big. Unlike your younger brother and sister, I don't even have to help you put your seat belt on when you jump into the car now. When I look into the future, I'm so excited for you. I'm so excited about all the people you will meet and all the things you will discover about this amazing world God has given us to take care of.

By now, if you have been reading the other letters I have written to your brothers and sister, you will have a pretty good idea that some people you meet will see the world completely different to the way you see it. They will even see themselves as completely different from the way you see them too. Not everyone will share your thoughts about God, about the world, about where we came from and where we are going. Therefore, not everyone will think about the meaning and purpose of their life like you do either.

I'm glad that it is your birthday tomorrow, because I get to write to you about the best and most important gift that God has ever given to the world. It is of course His Son, Jesus. Many people will not agree even on this simple point. Many people will disagree that God, if He is real at all, is a giving god. If they think He does exist, they will probably think that He is not a giver. They will think that He is a taker. Many people think that He only wants to take away our fun and our freedom. If He gives us anything, He simply waits until we mess up and then He can give us something from His long list of punishments.

When it comes to enjoying life and being who you want to be, then God only gets in the way for so many people. But, Abigail, this is only because, for so many people, they have never seriously looked at Jesus. In fact, many of your friends are growing up in a world where they will only think of a famous soccer player in one of the English football teams when they hear the name Jesus.

But here is perhaps the biggest and most important thing I'm going to say in any of these letters to you all. Please think about this over and over again when it comes to making your big decisions in life, like what job to do, where to live, who to marry (if you ever want to get married … though not for a very, very, very long time …). All these are very big and important questions indeed. But there is one other thing to see, more important than all the rest. Here it is: you will never truly understand who you are, until you are clear on who

Jesus really is. If you were allowed to draw on books (which you are not) then I would be telling you to take out your pencil, pen and the brightest coloured felt tip and to underline, circle and highlight that last sentence. So let me say it again, just so you are sure that I mean what I say: you will never truly understand who you are, until you are clear on who Jesus is.

This is not the place or the time to start telling you everything that the Bible says about Jesus. That is why we read our Bibles and pray to God as much as we can. Not that we get to do this every day, because one of your brothers or sister is usually screaming, crying or trying to destroy something around the house, but we do try. And when we open our Bibles it is important to remember that God has written it for us to show us what's important and exactly what He thinks about Jesus. All I have space to say now is that the Jesus of the Bible is God's most precious possession and His most wonderful gift to the world. So no matter what else you decide to do with your life, please make sure that you know for yourself who He is. He alone is able to make sense of this world, of your world, and He, alone, can take even our greatest difficulties and problems and use them for our ultimate good. For sure, one of the first questions that God will ever ask anyone who has ever lived is 'What did you think about my Son?'

I honestly do think that if more and more people took the time to see Jesus for who He really is, then they would be able to understand more and more about themselves and about this world. This is true for boys who are confused or don't want to be boys, and girls who don't want to grow up to be women. But it is not

49

only true for them. This is a problem everyone you will ever meet will be trying to solve. And we will not find the answer to who we are by looking inward at ourselves or by changing outwardly how we look. Even if we do manage to fix how we look and feel happier in ourselves, if we continue to rely on ourselves for that happiness it will never last. We need to rely on Him.

When you were very young, a lot younger than seven years old, you used to love the nursery rhymes that I would say, or try and sing to you. One of those is the famous story of Humpty Dumpty. Remember how it goes? About the big egg who fell off the wall? And it ends with the sad news, 'All the king's horses and all the king's men, couldn't put Humpty together again.' Poor old Humpty just had to lie there, broken. It's not a very happy ending, but it gets even more sad when you consider that this is like all our lives. Remember, in this world, there are indeed moments of real beauty and laughter, but in the end we are all broken and no matter how hard we try, or whoever else we turn to in this world, no one can put us back together again. All the king's horses and all the king's men are completely useless. The only person who can, the one person we all so desperately need is the King. He is the only one who can fix us, put us back together again and eventually one day make us perfect. Abigail, His name is Jesus, He's the real king. Not the stuff of nursery rhymes or fairy tales, but God's chosen ruler who came into our world to rescue us, and who continues to change people's lives right up until today. So at the risk of having to suffer another rolling of your eyes, let me say it one more time: you are never going to make sense of who you are, until you see Him for who He really is.

Happy Birthday, darling.

Love,

Dad

~ Genesis 3:14-15; 2 Samuel 7:12-16; Psalm 2; Isaiah 9:6-7, 53:1-12; Daniel 9:13-14; John 8:56-59, 10:10; Acts 4:12; 2 Corinthians 14-21; Ephesians 2:1-10; Revelation 1:12-18 ~

● ● ● ● ● ● ● ● ● ● ● ● ● ● ●

This letter really takes us to the heart of how transgenderism can actually deepen our understanding of the gospel. The clarion call of this book is simply that no one is ever going to make sense of who they really are, until they see Jesus for who He really is. When viewed from this perspective transgenderism is simply another cry of our broken human hearts to try and make sense of this world and ourselves in it. In this sense it is no better or worse than any other deep-seated human sin (act of rebellion) against our gracious God. It will not deliver on all its promises for those who fully embrace it, and it will not banish anyone completely from God's forgiveness and everlasting love, when they finally bow the knee to Jesus.

How to begin a conversation:

●   *Talk about who your favourite super heroes were growing up and what you really liked about them, but then point out their failures and weaknesses. We all know we need saving, and there is one real super hero who has no weaknesses and never once failed. Amazingly, He wants to know us and be our friend too.*

- *Who do your children think are important people in their lives and why? What do they then think about Jesus?*

Prayer ideas:

Dear God, thank you for Jesus, your Son, my Saviour, and help me to live with him as my Lord. Amen.

8
Cross-Dressing

Dear Caleb,

Although you yourself were never really into dressing up, you have certainly seen your little brother and sisters get lots of fun out of being someone completely different. Daniel, being the youngest, is prey to his older sisters who have recently discovered make-up and like to practise on him! Daniel himself is actually quite happy to play along and gets a big kick out of sporting blue nails, a nurse's dress and his Bob the Builder wellie boots. These are the pictures your mum and I will use in future years to blackmail him into obedience!

But in truth, Caleb, even when we grow up we all still wear certain masks sometimes. I don't mean anything like a Halloween mask or like the ones you wear for fancy dress. These masks that adults sometimes have to wear are a lot more difficult to spot, because they don't involve make-up or anything to cover your face. But just sometimes adults have to pretend that everything is fine, when actually, in reality, they may feel terrible. This is part of what it means to grow up, as we learn to think of others before ourselves. Remember how we have talked about this before, and we've agreed that rather than us being under the control of our feelings it is a lot better that they are under our control. That way, we will actually be able to think about others and their needs first, rather than simply being carried away by our own wants and desires.

However, Caleb, this way of thinking and behaving today will be looked upon as being very strange indeed. Almost everything you watch, a lot of what you read, many of the conversations you have in the playground, and even your own thinking, will tell you that the opposite way to live is actually the best way to live. You will be told repeatedly that no matter what else you do in this life, you must make sure that you are happy, and that this happiness is possible only when you are true to who you want to be. But did you notice the huge problem with that last sentence? (Have another read of it.) The only person it is concerned about, and tells you that you must be concerned about, over and above everyone else … is yourself! Therein, Caleb, lies the source of almost every other problem, both big and small in the world. And sometimes, yes, some adults wear certain masks and say certain things, just to get their own way. You will need to weigh carefully what people say and do as you grow up. But think about this: if everyone thinks that they are the most important person in the world, then when even two people get together in a room, war is guaranteed to break out. You see and experience this almost on a daily basis when a full-scale assault is mounted between you and Clara simply to be in charge of the TV control.

By contrast then, the message of the whole Bible, and the God of the Bible Himself, is so different. This is what makes being a Christian one of the most exciting and yet one of the most challenging ways to live. Let me explain. This alternative way to live is most perfectly explained by the cross on which Jesus died. In your reading of the gospels, the life stories of Jesus, you've already seen how strong and powerful He is. Nothing or no one is able to stand against Him … from evil spirits and raging storms to sickness and even death itself. And yet the big surprise is at the end of the story we find Him on a cross, suffering and dying Himself! Now the big question must be why? And one of the most important verses in the whole Bible puts it so simply for us. It simply says, 'Christ died for our sins' (1 Cor. 15:3). It states the fact. He died. But it also explains what He was doing by dying. He died for or *because* of sins … and that makes His death completely different. Of course we will all die one day. This is evidence of God's punishment for not trusting Him. But if you are following carefully you'll be confused by this point … because you'll know the thing that makes Jesus so different is that He always trusted God His Father, He always, therefore, obeyed … He lived the perfect life and, therefore, did not deserve to die and suffer any punishment. So the question is still, why then did He die? And the answer is: not for His sins. He didn't have any. No, the great life-changing truth is that He died not for His own sins, but for the sin of the whole world. That means He died for your sin and for mine.

You're already familiar with the idea of a substitution. In rugby if a player gets injured or tired, then the coach can bring him off and send on another player in his place. This is what lies at the heart of the cross and the whole message of Christianity. Jesus was being punished for our sin, in our place, and amazingly what Jesus did there by dying on the cross was enough to cover every sin for every person forever. (You may want to re-read that last sentence too.) That means each and every day, when you or I sin, disobey God's Word, fail to trust Him or hurt other people, we now have good news to preach to ourselves!

Jesus died for my sin. The punishment I deserve has already been taken by another. Such an act of substitution is of course good news for everyone, Caleb. There is no one who could ever have deserved such an act of love. And yet this is the very reason why Jesus came; to die for our sin! No matter what our particular sins are, Jesus saw them and still died for them all.

This is completely and utterly life-changing, Caleb, and if you want the truth, I'm still working out what this means and trying to work it into my own life, day by day.

At the moment you are learning what metaphors are, so let me put a lot of them down all at once and mix them all together. If you take this into the centre of your life, if it is the fuel that you put into your engine, then although you will still be hurt and confused by the world, you will be able to weather every storm, knowing that you are loved by your Maker. It is this simple truth that, when properly understood, is life-changing for everyone.

And if you understand that you are loved with an everlasting love, then you can at last begin to serve other people, rather than use them for yourself.

One of the most graphic ways to remember all this, Caleb, might be to say that on the cross Jesus was stripped naked of His perfect life and covered by the smallest and stinkiest, to the most terrible, most awful sin that any of us could commit. In turn, if we agree that He did in fact do that and died for us, as we trust in Him, the opposite happens on our end. Amazingly, all of our sins, from the smallest white lie to the great big embarrassing ones, are washed clean away from us and God places the spotless, brilliantly perfect clothes of His Son on our backs. Meaning we are now welcomed by God into His family forever. It is in this sense, Caleb, that you might say that every Christian has actually undergone the ultimate experience of 'cross-dressing', but the only difference is that unlike Daniel's fun, this is for real and changes us forever.

At heart, this is what everyone is longing for Caleb, from the most content and self-satisfied adult, to every boy or girl you will meet who wants to change how they look and feel. We are all trying so hard to make ourselves acceptable to others and even to ourselves. But we will only ever enjoy this deep complete sense of acceptance when we look at the cross and see Jesus dying there in our place. It is the ultimate expression of everlasting love.

Take this to heart, my son, and it will bring glory to God, be for your eternal good, and fill your life with grace for others.

Lovingly,
Dad

~ Genesis 3:21; Exodus 12:1-28; Psalm 51, 103; Isaiah 52:13-53:12, 56:1-8; Mark 10:45; John 3:16 ~

● ● ● ● ● ● ● ● ● ● ● ● ● ● ●

Acceptance is central to those advocating for transgenderism in society today. But it is not only part of a public campaign, it is also deeply personal. In fact, again, acceptance is something that we all crave and long for. Those struggling with gender dysphoria have a more heightened awareness of this need, but it remains the same for us all. The dangerous thing is when we seek to find this acceptance either within ourselves, or from others in society. The only place we will find true and lasting acceptance is when we discover real and everlasting approval. The gospel says we don't deserve this, can never earn it, and certainly cannot merit it. This is the reason Jesus is such good news. It is the reason why His death is so central to God's story and what we all must acknowledge and trust if we are to know this acceptance and approval from God as a reality in our lives. He performed there the one complete, and all-sufficient, sacrifice for the sins of the whole world, and substituted His life for ours. I need this great act of love, just as much as my transgender friend does. In fact, it is something the whole world needs to hear about.

How to begin a conversation:

- *Since the sacrificial substitutionary death of Jesus is central to the good news, make the most of every opportunity to point out how Jesus' act of love and His substituting of Himself for us really is great news. We substitute so many things today: fake tan, footballers, plastic flowers … use the natural and obvious examples to work this into your child's heart and never be slow in pointing out why Jesus is the perfect and only substitute for us.*

- *Jesus' work on the cross is perfect and remains for all time the only way to God. On a trip to the beach, when playing in the sand, ask if this would be a good place to build a house. Try and show the analogy between building our lives on anything other than Jesus' finished work.*

Prayer ideas:

Lord Jesus, thank you so much for loving us so much that you died for us and stood in our place to take the punishment we deserved. Help us to always count on your great and everlasting work on the cross and to see ourselves covered by your life-giving death. Amen.

9
Frustrated Hope?

Dear Clara,

Sometimes even mummies and daddies worry! We sometimes worry about silly things, like what we are going to make for your dinner, and then sometimes we worry about bigger things, like the type of world that you are going to grow up in. You'll face problems I can't even imagine at the moment.

But at the moment you are four years old and as I think about the future, I love to hear all that you want to be. I love it that you want to be a doctor, Elsa from *Frozen* (but a good Elsa) and a butterfly. I simply love it that you think you can be whatever you want.

In these letters I've been writing about other boys and girls who want to grow up to become the opposite to the way they were born. As I have suggested, this is not just dressing up differently, it is not pretending. For many of them it is really scary and confusing and makes them, and their mummies and daddies, very worried. To make matters worse, if we were to bring God into their stories, they would say that God had made a terrible mistake and given them the wrong bodies. But as we read God's story, I hope you can see that God is not in the habit of making mistakes. He is not like us, we all make mistakes and mess up, but God never does. Even when it came to the death of His own Son, God had planned it. The worst possible thing happened to the best, the perfect Man, and He had planned even this a long, long time before it happened for our good.

Another problem we have is that because there is so much pain and sadness in the world, we think that God must not care, or He would do something about it.

Now the first thing to say is that this world is not the way it was originally built. Remember in the beginning God gave Adam and Eve a great home, but they didn't want God to be in control. The world now is in a bit of a mess, but that's not because God messed it up. We did, and we continue to mess it up every day.

It is a little bit like your bedroom. Your mummy and daddy try to keep things in order. We know that there is a place for everything and if they stayed in their place, then it would be a happy bedroom. But then, when some of your friends come over, like Chippy, what do you do to it? You think that it's a good idea to throw things around, make a mess and pull it apart. Our world is like your bedroom. In the beginning God put it together perfectly, but then we decided we knew better and continually throw things around and make something of a mess of it. So when it comes then to using it for what it has been designed for we get very frustrated, just like when you try to get into bed and go to sleep after one of your dance parties. Your pillow is missing, your covers are on the floor and your little ponies are already sleeping under your mattress.

So secondly, this world is full of frustrations! Here is the hard truth, Clara. You are not going to grow up to be a butterfly. You are not going to have the ice powers of Elsa, even if you wanted to use them for the good of others, and you might not even be a doctor. I know that this is hard to believe at the moment, and I certainly want you to have fun thinking that you could be all these things. I wanted to be Superman when I was growing up, and actually jumped off a wall thinking I could fly, but there are just some rules that can't be changed. I was very angry at gravity after I jumped off that wall as a little boy, but as I have got older, I can see that gravity is actually quite a good thing and without it, life in this world would indeed be all over the place.

Now I know that as a parent it is easy for me to say this when talking to you about your wishes and dreams. It is not so easy for other mummies and daddies to tell their children that they cannot grow up to be who they think they should become. But all of our tears, our disappointments and frustrations (and there will be many, many more for you as you grow up) point us all to the simple fact that this is not the world that any of us want. If we try and change it in the wrong direction and completely ignore the way it has been made then we will only run into more problems. If we try and change ourselves in the wrong direction and completely ignore the way we have been made, although it might seem right and good now, in the future we will only run into more and more problems too.

What I need you to remember from this letter is that this is not God's fault. He did not and does not make any mistakes. Boys and girls who feel that they have been given the wrong bodies perhaps feel the messiness of this world more than most, but if they then try and fix themselves by simply doing what seems to be best in their own eyes right now, they are doing nothing more than rearranging the mess. Life is still going to be very messy for them, as it is for us all.

But perhaps even more importantly than anything else, although this mess was not His making, God has done something about it. You see, instead of turning away and giving up on it, He loved it so much that He actually entered into our mess. He suffered and died, because someone had to be punished for the mess we've made. But then He did not stay dead. Three days later He rose from the grave to give the world a huge and wonderful hope: that one day He would fix it all.

Before that great and awesome day, what He calls us all to do is to trust Him. I so long that you would do this: simply agree that He does know best even if you can't understand all His ways. His promise is that if we build our lives on His Word, then we will be able to make more sense of our mess and frustrations here and now and that one day, a long, long time from now, we will look back and agree that He made no mistakes.

I know that this is a really big thing to understand right now, but again, if you have any questions about anything at all, then please do just ask me.

I love you so much,
Dad

~ Psalm 13; Isaiah 25:6-9; John 8:10-11; Acts 1:1-11; Romans 8:18-25; 2 Corinthians 4:16-18; Philippians 3:20-4:1; 1 Thessalonians 1:9-10; 2 Peter 3:8-13 ~

● ● ● ● ● ● ● ● ● ● ● ● ● ● ●

This chapter uses the conclusion of the Bible's story (the new heavens and new earth) as a backdrop while at the same time trying to move the emphasis more onto the pastoral implications. Namely, while we wait for Jesus' return, there is much that is frustrating in this world. In fact, such frustration is an indication to all that we are made for something better than this world.

How to begin a conversation:

- *When you or your wife get sick or when you as a family experience some sort of grief, speak openly about the brokenness of this world and the need for God to do something about it.*
- *When you experience something great together, like a wonderful meal, explain that this world is not perfect and yet it can still be so enjoyable … so how much greater will heaven be.*
- *Take the time to talk about the different ways people try to make things perfect here and now … even how they try to make themselves perfect, but then help your children realise that this won't work. We must wait for Jesus' return.*

Prayer ideas:

Dear God, this is a beautiful, but deeply broken world. Help us to live here and now as those who are going to be with you in heaven forever. Amen.

10
Who Are You Going to Follow?

Dear Daniel,

These letters have been about a subject that you know nothing about yet. For you, life is about fun, food and finding ways to annoy your older brother and sisters. And yet, even you know what it feels like when you cannot get your own way. Your mummy and I have gone through the same routine with you, as we had to do with Caleb, Abigail and Clara and ask you repeatedly, 'Who is the boss around here?' You have cuteness on your side, so when you answered the first couple of times that 'Daniel is boss', I had to turn away and smile. You have learned to say, however, and occasionally even give-in and admit, that actually Mummy and Daddy are the bosses in the family. We'll just have to wait and see for how long you toe that line.

Behind the really hard and heartbreaking stories of boys and girls who don't like the way they have been made is this big question as to who is really in charge around here?

Daniel, as I said in some of my earlier letters to your brother and sisters you will have to answer this one question for yourself over and over again as you grow up in life. Answering it correctly will not always just be a matter of deciding between right and wrong. It certainly will involve that, but you will also need to see that by agreeing with one person instead of another, you are actually submitting to their way of thinking. This will shape your life, perhaps forever.

When it comes to some subjects, especially transgenderism, it will seem that you will be faced with so many different, opposing ideas, and like in a game of soccer, each opposing team will be trying to score more goals to show you that they really are the better team.

One thing is very clear already, however, if you take a good hard look at the team who say that boys and girls should be allowed to be whoever they want to become. Already, for many of them, if you disagree with them, they do not just want to score a goal against you, they actually want to take you out of the game. They want to stop you from playing completely, and are not interested in your team or anything you have to say. Now, of course, not all their team members are like this, but many of them are. In fact it can get so bad that they will even throw members of their own team off the pitch if they should not play according to their rules.

On their team, in defence, they have experts who produce lots of evidence. Some of this evidence will be very convincing. Many of these experts are doctors and have written many books on this subject. Please consider carefully all that they have to say. However, please also try to ask the question that your brother and sisters love to ask at the moment, 'Why?' Why are these experts saying what they are saying? Sometimes they are not always simply giving you the facts or the most up-to-date discoveries.

They also have a very strong midfield position called 'The Majority'. That sounds more impressive than it really is. If you have the majority of anything, it simply means that you have more of that one thing than someone else has. For those who want boys and girls to decide who they should be, they point to the number of people who think they are right and they say that 'The Majority' of people are on their side. This is a very important point so listen carefully. They may in fact be right on this. Many people, perhaps even most people, might agree with them, but this does not mean then that those who disagree are actually wrong. This is a bit of a silly example, but imagine that a whole bunch of aliens came down to earth and they thought that their right hand was actually their left hand and their left hand was in fact their right hand. Would we change the way we think? Probably not. But then imagine that they brought all their friends, so that there were now actually more aliens on planet earth than humans. In other words they would be in the majority and we would be in the minority. Would we now be convinced that what we have always known as our right hand should now in fact become our left hand? Again, probably not. Simply because a whole lot of people start saying that the opposite way of living is now right, does not make those who disagree with them wrong.

The star strikers of the whole team, however, are those who are held up to be the success stories of transgenderism. These are the people who are now living happy and free-er lives because they were allowed to change themselves to be who they always wanted to become. For some this is true, but please remember that it is not true for all of them. For some of them, they carry now a whole new set of disappointments and hurts. Some may even carry deep and painful regrets and have nowhere or no one left to turn to. They may have been convinced by the experts and carried along by the crowd. This is why it is so important that no matter who you meet, no matter how they look, that you see them as people, made by God and loved deeply by Him.

As I said the Bible for centuries has been doing more good in the world than is often admitted. Again today it is seen as actually being the source of lots of evil and hatred. Of course there are some people who don't understand the Bible and do hurtful things in the name of Jesus, but when you properly understand it, the Bible says we are to 'overcome evil with good' (Rom. 12:21). That at least means that how we treat those who disagree and oppose us matters. Jesus even went on record to say that we are to love our enemies and pray for those who persecute us.

And you do need to know, Daniel, that you probably will lose friends, suffer rejection and even find yourself sometimes all alone if you refuse to go along with the crowd. This will be terribly painful and you will be tempted to throw the whole lot in. There will even be many who say they are following Jesus and who still say that it is okay to live according to our feelings. These people are the most confusing and in the greatest danger of all. Jesus talked about many people who would come and claim to be His friend but continue to agree with the ways of the world. Treat them gently, but do not go along with them in their thinking and message.

In one of the most staggering things that Jesus (a man who positively oozed love) said, He reminded His followers that 'a servant is not greater than his master. If they persecuted me, they will also persecute you' (John 15:20). So don't be surprised, but also do not start to shout them down either. Instead speak the truth with compassion but without compromise.

Daniel, your mummy and I have made the decision to follow Him, to trust Him and that, we know, will mean that sometimes the world will think of us as its enemy. It is not an easy road to travel and it is likely to get worse. If you decide to do the same, please remember that He loves you and will never leave you. By His Spirit, Jesus has even promised to work within us, to make us more like Him, to *trans*form us so completely He can only describe it as in terms of us being *'born again'*; that is being given a brand new start and a life-changing relationship with God. Stay strong and press on, pointing everyone you meet to Him.

With all my love,
Dad

~ Proverbs 12:10, 15; Mark 8:34-38; John 17:14-19;
1 Peter 1:17-21; Jude 17-25 ~

• • • • • • • • • • • • • •

Finally, to wrap things up we look at the need to critically engage with our culture, while showing compassion to those who are lost. This chapter aims to give Christian parents some more courage to their convictions. The world is at a loss. This issue is another example of our need for clarity. Authority in general in the Western world is crumbling—politically, socially, medically. One authority has stood the test of time and has done more good in the world than perhaps any other. Rather than building on the sand, build our lives on the sure foundation.

How to begin a conversation:

- *Playing the 'why' game is always great fun—until it just becomes annoying—but your children love asking that question. Ultimately when it comes down to doing what someone else says there is a huge element of trust involved. Help them to see that God is perfectly trustworthy and more than this is the fact that He loves us too.*

- *Tell your children simply that everyone they ever meet is living a certain way because they are trusting someone. We take tablets from the doctor because we trust them. We get on an aeroplane because we trust the pilot. Other people might simply be trusting themselves in the way they behave. The question is, who will we trust?*

Prayer ideas:

Thank you so much that we can trust you, God. Thank you that you proved your trustworthiness by sending Jesus. Help us today to show we trust you by the way we live. Amen.

11
Excursus: A Short Conversation During a Car Journey Home from School

During a recent car journey home on school pickup, Caleb brought up an encounter that we had had just the previous day in the town where we live. By all accounts it is a small and insignificant town, but both he and Abigail noticed a man who was quite obviously wearing some items of women's clothing.

The next day Caleb brought this up in conversation. He asked very simply, why that man wanted to wear women's clothes. I didn't actually see the individual concerned as I was chasing Clara up the street and trying to keep her from playing with the traffic. The person concerned may or may not have been fully transgender, but it was enough to make my children stop and stare.

In response to Caleb's question this is the approach I took, summarising some of the thinking of this book.

'Caleb,' I said, 'there are some things that you are going to have to figure out as you grow up and one of them is how to think about and live beside people who are very different to you. You see the wonderful thing about this world, is that God has made it so full of lots of different types of people. So the first thing you're going to have to do is to stop and remember that no matter who they are that God made them and that He loves them.'

This seemed to be within Caleb's orbit and so we moved on. I slowed down slightly because the car journey home is not that long.

'Secondly then, Caleb,' I said, 'if we are going to follow Jesus, then we will want to treat everyone as Jesus would treat them.'

'OK.'

'And what that means, Caleb, is being kind and welcoming and warm in our actions and words towards them.'

I'm thinking, so far so good …

'But it will also mean, Caleb, that we cannot agree with everyone in how they want to live. If a person is really greedy then Jesus would not say that that was OK and leave them to go on being greedy. He would love them by telling them that only in a relationship with Him will they ever be satisfied and then change their greediness into generosity. And the same is true for men who want to become women and women who want to become men. Jesus would love them, absolutely, but that does not mean He would agree that the way they see themselves is right and that the changes they want to make are really for their greater happiness.'

I put on the indicator, turning into our house. I'm thinking that there is so much more to say, but I need to help Caleb see that everyone, from those with even mild self-discontentment and gender-dysphoria, right down to him, the most sensitive, caring and yet at times completely self-absorbed little boy you could ever meet, needs to come to terms with this …

'Lastly, Caleb, and this is the most important thing to always remember. Never forget,' I say, trying to underline and highlight it all at once, 'never forget that they, like you, will never understand who they really are, until they see Jesus for who He really is.'

And that's it. Engine off, and even before I unbuckle myself, he's out and away, leaving his school bag and lunch box in the footwell, chasing bubbles that his brother and sisters are blowing in the garden. He's gone … and I'm left thinking, 'What on earth is he going to do about all that he will face in a world where the only hope, the only One who, can actually make sense of this life, is so often the last place, the last person, they turn to.'

Epilogue:
A Prayer of a Dad for his Children

Heavenly Father,

Thank you so much that regardless of the time or how tired I am, I can come to you, confident that you hear and care. Thank you that nothing is outside your control and that no matter how bad things appear to me, nothing or no one is beyond your transforming power and redeeming love.

I want to thank you tonight especially for the wonderful gift of family life, with all of its thrills and spills. In your wisdom you have been pleased to give us four beautiful little children, who ensure that life is never dull. You made them, you alone perfectly know them and you have loved them so much as to give your Only Son for them. I pray that they will grow up to know you, trustingly follow Jesus, and keep in step with your Spirit as they hold fast to your Word.

Please help me as their dad to always love them and care enough to listen to them, to have fun with them and enjoy their company at the various stages they are all at. And please help me as their dad to love them enough to be clear with them about the things that really matter in life too.

As they grow up help them to enjoy who you have made them to be. May they be kind, may they be loving and may they be selfless and helpful to everyone they meet. Please keep them from simply following the crowd, and instead to be men and women of character, full of compassion as well as deep conviction about your truth. Give them more light and understanding about You than I possibly ever will have, and then give them the courage to walk in a manner worthy of their calling. When they do meet with disappointment or sadness about themselves, or in others, may they not despair, but instead grow in their need for Jesus and in their desire to become more like Him.

I pray this especially in relation to the world's confusing messages about what it means to be a man or a woman today. May they see their bodies, as well as their minds and skills, as gifts from You, and may they not seek to find fulfilment in themselves or true freedom apart from You, but instead, may they be fully satisfied with you and live therefore totally for You.

Thank you, our great God, that you have promised one day to bring to completion every good work you have started in us. Thank you for raising your Son from the dead to give us new birth into a living hope. Thank you that nothing can separate us from your love that is for us in Christ Jesus. And may we as a family then, be increasingly shaped by your faithfulness, your power and your love, as we seek to urge all those whom we meet to place their personal confidence, not in